Help Me **Understand**

Why Is
Cheating
Wrong?

Christine Honders

PowerKiDS press™

NEW YORK

Published in 2019 by The Rosen Publishing Group, Inc.
29 East 21st Street, New York, NY 10010

First Edition

Editor: Greg Roza
Book Design: Rachel Rising

Photo Credits: Cover, FatCamera/E+/Getty Images; p. 4 Cristian Zamfir/Shutterstock.com; p. 5 stockfour/Shutterstock.com; p. 6 DoublePHOTO studio/Shutterstock.com; p. 7 Suzanne Tucker/Shutterstock.com; p. 9 espies/Shutterstock.com; p. 11 LightField Studios/Shutterstock.com; p. 12 Mega Pixel/Shutterstock.com; p. 13 Ermolaev Alexander/Shutterstock.com; p. 15 Monkey Business Images/Shutterstock.com; p. 16 Raksha Shelare/Shutterstock.com; p. 17 Syda Productions/Shutterstock.com; p. 18 Photographee. eu/Shutterstock.com; p. 19 Lisa F. Young/Shutterstock.com; p. 20 AngieYeoh/Shutterstock.com; p. 21 fizkes/Shutterstock.com; p. 22 sashahaltam/Shutterstock.com.

Cataloging-in-Publication Data

Names: Honders, Christine.
Title: Why Is cheating wrong? / Christine Honders.
Description: New York : PowerKids Press, 2019. | Series: Help me understand | Includes glossary and index.
Identifiers: ISBN 9781538348123 (pbk.) | ISBN 9781538348147 (library bound) | ISBN 9781538348130 (6 pack)
Subjects: LCSH: Conduct of life–Juvenile literature. | Cheating–Juvenile literature. | Honesty–Juvenile literature.
Classification: LCC BJ1631.H66 2019 | DDC 179'.8–dc23

Manufactured in the United States of America

CPSIA Compliance Information: Batch #CWPK19. For Further Information contact Rosen Publishing, New York, New York at 1-800-237-9932

Contents

What's Wrong with Cheating?

Has anyone ever tried to copy your paper during a test? If they did, it probably made you upset. You might have thought that it wasn't fair. Trying to copy someone else's work is a form of cheating.

Sometimes cheating doesn't seem like a big deal. You might be losing at a board game with your friends. Maybe they won't notice if you move your piece one extra square. But cheating is never OK, even if it's just a game.

When kids cheat, it's not fair to the other kids who studied for the test.

5

Cheating Is Lying

Cheating is when a person breaks a rule in a **dishonest** way, often to get something they want. Cheating can happen anywhere: at home, at school, or during games.

If you play a sport, such as basketball, you're supposed to join a team with other kids your age. It wouldn't be fair if an older kid lied about their age and signed up to play on a team for younger kids. The older kid would be cheating so they could win.

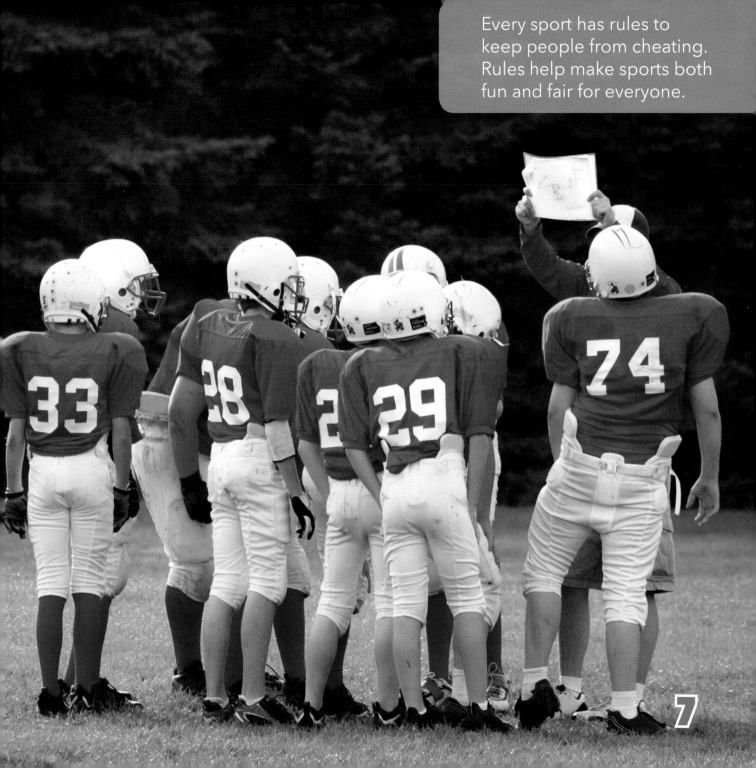

Every sport has rules to keep people from cheating. Rules help make sports both fun and fair for everyone.

Ways People Cheat

People can cheat in many different ways. The Internet makes it very easy to cheat. Some kids look up other people's work on the Internet and copy it. Then they give it to their teacher and pretend it's their own. That kind of cheating is called **plagiarism**.

Breaking the rules of a game is also cheating. There are rules so that everyone has a fair chance to win. When someone cheats and always wins, the game isn't fun for the other players anymore.

Taking someone else's work and pretending it's your own isn't just cheating, it's stealing.

9

Why Do People Cheat?

Some kids are so busy they don't think they have time to study. They think they have to cheat to get good grades. Other kids just don't feel like doing the work. They would rather watch TV than study.

Some kids feel like they won't do well unless they cheat. They might think their parents or the leader of their sports team will be unhappy if they don't win or do well on a test. No matter what the reason is, there's never a good reason to cheat.

Someone who thinks they can't get good grades unless they cheat should talk to their teacher or parents. Working on the problem is better than cheating.

Cheating in Class

Cheating in school might seem like the easiest way to get good grades. But cheating can make school harder. If you cheat on a test, you'll have the right answers once, but you haven't really learned anything. You won't know how to pass the next test. You may think you have to cheat again!

School is a place to learn. It's better to find out and understand the reasons behind the answers. If you cheat in school, you're not really learning.

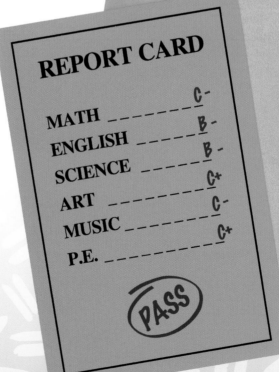

REPORT CARD

MATH _ _ _ _ _ _ _ _ C-
ENGLISH _ _ _ _ _ _ B-
SCIENCE _ _ _ _ _ B-
ART _ _ _ _ _ _ _ _ C+
MUSIC _ _ _ _ _ _ C-
P.E. _ _ _ _ _ _ _ _ C+

PASS

You're not helping your friend if you let them copy your paper. They're not learning anything.

13

Cheating During Games

It's **tempting** to cheat during a game because winning is so much fun! But the rest of the players are working hard and trying to win **honestly**. They won't have a fair chance to win if someone else cheats.

Some people cheat at games because they're unhappy with themselves. They think that winning will make them feel better. But the other players might get angry and not want to play with them anymore. Then the cheater may feel worse.

You might think you're helping your team by cheating. But you're really letting your teammates down. They could get in trouble too, and they won't know if they could have won without cheating.

→

If You're Caught

If you're caught cheating on a test, you could be given a zero for a grade. The teacher will probably tell your parents. They'll be upset and think they can't trust you. You might feel **embarrassed**.

The worst part about getting caught cheating is that other people might lose respect for you. They won't trust you, and they might decide that you're not a good friend. They might not want to spend time with you anymore.

If someone wants to copy your answers, you should tell your teacher.

17

What If They Never Find Out?

Even if someone cheats and doesn't get caught, it's still the wrong thing to do. Cheating often makes the person feel **anxious** or **guilty**. The cheater may always worry that they'll be found out.

Cheating really hurts the cheater. When someone cheats, they're saying, "I don't think I can do this fairly." They cheat because they don't believe they can do the work on their own. So, even if they aren't caught, cheating makes people feel bad about themselves.

If you cheat once, the teacher will think you're not honest and will watch you closely next time.

19

Making the Right Choice

Almost everyone thinks about cheating at some point. Most people don't cheat, though, because they know it's wrong. But others start cheating and think that they can't stop. If you've cheated before, it's not too late. You can choose to stop and work for things instead. You'll feel proud of yourself because you played fair.

Kids who don't stop cheating might cheat for the rest of their lives. Adults who cheat can get into a lot more trouble than getting bad grades. Cheating at their job could get them fired!

Cheating can become a bad **habit**. It's up to you to decide to stop and do the right thing.

21

Cheaters Never Win

Sometimes it seems like cheaters get what they want. They don't work very hard and always win. It's important to remember that cheaters win because they aren't playing fair. Cheaters aren't really winners because they lied to get what they wanted.

A real winner is someone who works hard, plays fair, and follows the rules. When they get good grades and win at sports, it's because they earned it. Isn't that better than cheating?

Glossary

anxious: Afraid or nervous about what might happen.

dishonest: Saying things that aren't true.

embarrassed: The state of feeling foolish in front of others.

guilty: Feeling bad because you've done something wrong.

habit: A way of behaving, often again and again.

honestly: In a truthful way.

plagiarism: The act of stealing someone else's work and pretending it's your own.

tempting: Causing a strong wish to have or do something.

Index

Websites

Due to the changing nature of Internet links, PowerKids Press has developed an online list of websites related to the subject of this book. This site is updated regularly. Please use this link to access the list: www.powerkidslinks.com/help/cheating